Oliver Onion

The Onion Who Learns to Accept and Be Himself

Oliver Onion

The Onion Who Learns to Accept and Be Himself

Written and Illustrated by Diane Murrell

APC

Autism Asperger Publishing Co.
P.O. Box 23173
Shawnee Mission, KS 66283-0173
www.asperger.net

© 2004 by Autism Asperger Publishing Company
P.O. Box 23173
Shawnee Mission, KS 66283-0173
www.asperger.net

Publisher's Cataloging-in-Publication
(Provided by Quality Books, Inc.)

Murrell, Diane.
  Oliver Onion : the onion who learns to accept and be
himself / Diane Murrell.
    p. cm.
  SUMMARY: Unhappy with the way he looks, Oliver Onion
decides to change his looks in hopes of becoming
happier. He manages to wrap himself in an orange peel
hoping that will help, but he soon realizes that it's
best to stay who he is.
  Audience: K-4.
  Library of Congress Control Number: 2004112002
  ISBN 1-931282-64-1

  1. Self-acceptance—Juvenile fiction.
[1. Self-acceptance—Fiction.]   I. Title.

PZ7.M9666Oli 2004   [E]
                            QBI33-2106

This book is designed in Kristen ITC.

Managing Editor: Kirsten McBride

Printed in Korea

For Pippi Longstocking (a.k.a. Jessica Duncan),

her incorrigible cohorts, Kirsten and Naomi Duncan

and baby Eva

An onion is a bulb, not the kind that gives a glow, but the kind you plant and grow. You cannot plant a light bulb – it needs electricity. In the ground you cannot find plugs and switches, just slugs and ditches.

This is Oliver. Oliver is an onion. You can tell that he is an onion by his smooth, shiny skin and his untidy tuft of hair. When you look at him, you might think Oliver is upside down, but he is really downside up. Everybody agrees that he is a very handsome onion, but Oliver does not like the way he looks. He wants to look different.

Upside down

Downside up

Oliver has been dug up from the field and taken to the farmer's market. He is lying in the onion box talking to Peter the Potato in the box next to him.

Looking around
at the other fruits and vegetables,
Oliver burst out, "Oh, Peter,
do you ever wish you
looked different?
Perhaps long and orange like
those carrots, or red like
an apple — or maybe yellow and curved like that banana?"

"No!" Peter answered, "I am just fine the way I am — round and brown. You look good
too, Oliver. All the different shapes and colors are wonderful, including yours and mine."
But Oliver didn't listen.

After a while Oliver heard one of the other onions complain about the cold coming through a hole in the part of the box where she was lying. Hearing about the hole gave him an idea! He asked the onion if she would like to change places with him. "Okay," she answered, and soon the two had switched places.

Through the hole in the box, Oliver watched a girl eating an orange. "Mmm! Delicious!" she said, enjoying the cool, juicy fruit. When done, she threw the orange peel on the ground.

"Perhaps I should be an orange instead of a carrot, an apple, or a banana," thought Oliver. "I would look different and that would change me into a new person with a new life. And someone would call me delicious!"

Happy with his new idea, Oliver wasted no time!! He squeezed through the tiny hole in the box, let himself fall to the ground and rolled over to the orange peel the girl had thrown away.

After a quick inspection, Oliver pushed his way into the peel and began to wrap it around himself. "This is the perfect fit for an onion who wants to be an orange," he thought.

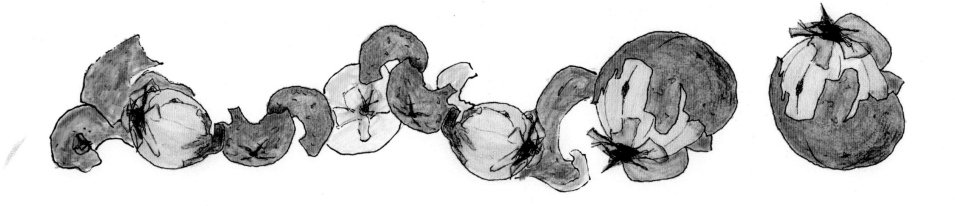

From inside his new orange cover, Oliver peeped out, making sure that no one would step on him. But suddenly, a BIG STRONG HAND GRABBED HIM and put him in a box full of oranges.

Oliver immediately realized that Oratio, a very large orange, was in charge. "Well, oranges," Oratio said, "fine work! You looked very handsome and fetched a good price. Tomorrow we will be taken to a big store. Now let's get some sleep before the long journey."

The oranges quieted down, snuggling close together to go to sleep. But Oliver couldn't fall asleep. He felt uncomfortable – he was wrapped too tightly in the orange peel.

Waiting for a while, he opened up a tiny gap in his orange cover and took a long, deep breath. After making sure that all the oranges were fast asleep, he opened up a larger gap. Still he was uncomfortable. The inside of the orange peel felt scratchy against his own smooth skin. Besides, it was too hot to be inside two skins – his own and the orange peel.

Oliver was so uncomfortable that he tossed and turned all night – even in his sleep. His flipping and flopping even woke up many of the oranges, but Oliver slept on.

"Look at him!" cried Jorge, a bright young orange, pointing at the sleeping Oliver. "He's not an orange!" He nudged Oliver, "Wake up!"

Oliver woke up instantly and cautiously peeped through the gap in the orange peel. Every orange in the box was now watching him, waiting to see what he would do. Oliver froze. He was frightened. It was not fun pretending to be an orange when he really wasn't.

As he saw Oratio coming closer, Oliver began to tremble. Feeling totally miserable, he decided now was the time to face the truth – he was an onion, and he could never change into anything else!

Slowly he lifted the orange peel surrounding him and said quietly, "I am Oliver, the onion." The orange peel fell away, uncovering an untidy tuft of hair and a sad, timid face. "I hid in this peel so I could be like you," he stuttered.

"But you are not like us," said Oratio. "WE are ORANGES. YOU are NOT! Besides, you have to leave now because WE are going on a very important trip to a very important store tomorrow and WE need OUR sleep."

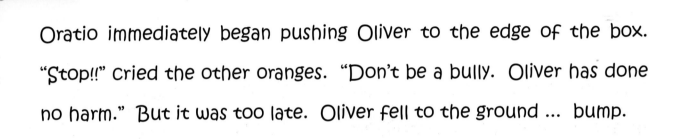

Oratio immediately began pushing Oliver to the edge of the box.
"Stop!!" cried the other oranges. "Don't be a bully. Oliver has done
no harm." But it was too late. Oliver fell to the ground ... bump.

"Bye, Oliver," the other oranges whispered fondly.

"Go to sleep, oranges," grumbled Oratio. Then he threw the orange
peel on the ground after Oliver.

Oliver rolled away from the box and lay totally still. It began to turn cold and dark, so he wrapped himself up in the orange peel to stay warm even though he knew he would not be comfortable. For a moment he lay gazing up at the stars. He was very tired. It was hard work for an onion to try to be an orange and to live in constant fear of being found out. It's always difficult to be to be something you are not!

Soon he fell asleep on the roadside.

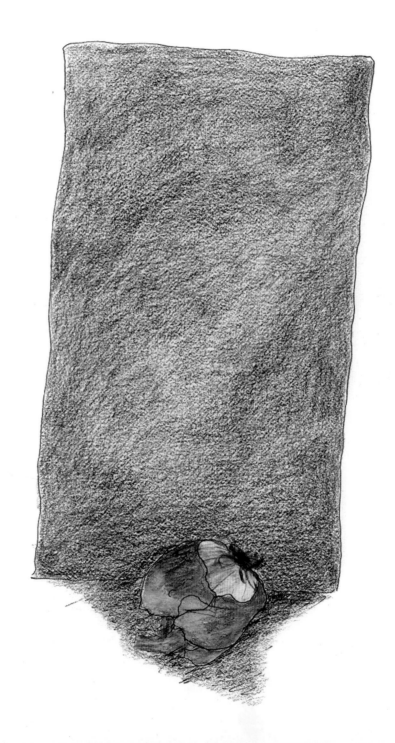

Oliver woke up to a new day. The sun was smiling down on him. Oliver gleamed in the morning light. He looked at the discarded orange peel. It had already begun to shrivel and wrinkle, and its bright orange color was fading. It was no longer a wonderful disguise.

"Hey, hey!" Oliver suddenly heard somebody yelling and looked up. Moving past him in a large truck, all the oranges were peering over their box, smiling at him. "Oh look how handsome you are," they called out. "You gleam brightly in the morning sun; you don't need our "PEEL" to give you "APPEAL." You shine beautifully.

Hearing their kind words, Oliver looked down at his rounded tummy and saw his body shining with glimmers of light. Once he had disliked himself, but now he was happy to be an onion. Happy to be himself. "I AM AN ONION," he said, "and an onion is all I want to be. Peter the Potato was right when he said that every shape and color is wonderful, including me!"

Happily, Oliver gave a little skip and
began to roll down the road. From now on,
he would like and accept himself and not try
to change into someone else.

THE END!!!

Discussion Guide

Oliver Onion is written for 4- to 10-year-olds. It is a book that children can read alone or that can be shared aloud. When asked what *they* think the story is about, children have initiated some very lively discussions that center on self-acceptance, self-respect and self-worth.

In addition to simply enjoying the story and the engaging illustrations, the story of Oliver Onion may be used to help children who struggle with issues of acceptance – whether accepting themselves or others. The story may be explored on several levels, from the very simple face value of an onion who is having a bad day and fakes being an orange, to the quite complex layers of struggle that some children encounter with various perceived or real inadequacies. These might include physical features, intelligence, loneliness, talents or personality traits.

The discussion categories listed below are not exhaustive but serve as jumping-off points for helping children to thoughtfully examine their thinking about self and others based on Oliver Onion's experiences.

Imagination and Generalization (Abstract Thinking Skills)
Giving children a vehicle for describing themselves, such as a fruit or vegetable in this context (it could be trains, cars or the child's hero), is often helpful as it removes them from the vulnerability of having to be too personal.

Sometimes children need help in taking a story or a situation and applying it to their own life (generalization).

- Which fruit or vegetable are you like? Why?
- Have you ever wished you were somebody else? Who? Why?
- What did Oliver learn? Do you know that? How/when might you use that knowledge?

"Never Judge a Book by Its Cover"… or an Onion by Its Skin …
This discussion topic is pretty obvious given Oliver's fate and should generate a lively discussion among children.

- Did lying and pretending to be someone else help Oliver?
- What happened when Oliver tried to be something he was not?
- What kind of trouble do people get into when they cannot be themselves?
- What does it mean when we say "Never judge a book by its cover"?
- Was Oliver judging other fruits or vegetables by their "cover"?
- Were any of the fruits and vegetables judging Oliver by his cover/looks?

Sensory Issues

Sensory integration problems can not only cause physical discomfort but may also lead to social skill difficulties. Aspects of Oliver's story open a door to discussing sensory problems that are an integral part of some children's lives. These include increased and decreased sensitivity to touch from friends, clothing and/or textures. They include sensitivity to taste, temperature, noise, smell, lighting, etc.

- Unlike Oliver, who is uncomfortable with the rough orange skin pressed against his own smooth skin, some children like to be wrapped up and feel heavy pressure. Discuss light touch and firm pressure.
- For kinesthetic learning, have the children touch a carrot, an apple, a banana, an onion, an orange, an orange peel, etc.
- Explore the meaning of descriptive words for each vegetable or fruit, such as smooth, shiny, delicious, handsome, noting where those adjectives might be useful to apply to humans.

Bullying

Although Oliver Onion is not primarily a story about bullying, the topic merits discussion in view of how Oratio treats Oliver. Given the widespread occurrence of bullying, any exploration should be solution-focused: how to handle it if it happens to you and how to report it if you see it happening to another person.

- Oratio is a bully in this story. What makes him a bully?
- Do you know anyone like that?
- The other oranges were upset when Oratio bullied, do you think bullies have many friends?
- What can you do if someone is mean to you?
- What can you do if you see someone being mean to another person?
- Did the oranges' kind words help Oliver?
- Do you use kind words to help people?

What Children Have Said

Many children who have listened to this story have given their opinion that appearance is not as important as what is on the inside. Oliver's focus is *be yourself!*

Below are several observations made by children in a fourth-grade class. They are reproduced here using their original spelling and wording.

Be greatful for what you have not what you want.
Don't be jelous about what you never had
Allan Binaisao

Be happy with yourself because you shine your own way, everyday.
It doesn't matter whats on the outside what counts is the inside,
Cassidy Smith

Others might have a gift you want, but you'll have a gift they want.
Even though you might think you're dull, you have something to share from what you think is dull.
Amy Durand

Be yourself
Don't go to hang with other crowd when your's
is just fine.   Khadesia

Learn to be yourself
                              Luis Ramirez

Someone shouldn't
try   to be who they aren't.
Be   yourself.
                    Kirk Murrell

Respect who you are not as anyone else ♡
Never be a orange when your perfect as an Orion.
                                    Lydia Gibson

Like yourself for who you are.
Don't be anything your not
                              Ryan williams